DUNDEE ON RECORD

Images of the Past

Prospectus Civitatis TAODUNI ab Oriente. The Prospect of y Town of DUNDEE from y East.

39.

View of Dundee from east, drawn by Captain John Slezer

This is one of the two perspectives of Dundee contained in Slezer's *Theatrum Scotiae* (*c.* 1693), the first topographical book published in Scotland to provide bird's-eye views of principal burghs, houses and gardens. Here the elongated east west layout, the harbour and some stone buildings are crearly evident; St Mary's Tower is still the dominant landmark (NMRS AND/850/3).

DUNDEE ON RECORD
Images of the Past

Photographs and Drawings in the National Monuments Record of Scotland

ISBN 0 11 494208 0

Cover illustrations
front High Street View from west (c1878)
back High Street 1992

CONTENTS

View of Dundee from the Law (c. 1878)
In this view, contained in an album of photographs taken mainly by the Dundee firm, Valentine, the mediaeval centre and St Mary's Tower are surrounded by a forest of smoking factory chimneys, tenements and other Victorian buildings. The Royal Infirmary is visible to the left of centre, and Dudhope Castle at far right. In the foreground, a villa is seen under construction immediately adjacent to open countryside (NMRS B41668; album 67).

PREFACE

This volume brings together a selection of photographs and drawings relating to the buildings and archaeological sites of City of Dundee District, drawn from the rich collections of material in the National Monuments Record of Scotland. These illustrations show the diversity of these collections, which embrace photographs and drawings of various dates, together with an extensive library of books and pamphlets. They also demonstrate the extent of NMRS coverage of one of Scotland's major cities, including its everyday building-types as well as its architectural set-pieces. The greatest emphasis falls naturally on the industries and buildings of the city's Victorian and Edwardian heyday, but there is also a wealth of material on earlier periods, from prehistoric to Georgian, and on the dramatic expansion and rebuilding which occurred in the 20th century. Many of these illustrations were used in an exhibition presented by RCAHMS as a contribution to Dundee's 1991 Octocentenary celebrations.

The greater part of the text was written and illustrations selected by Miles Horsey and edited by Geoffrey Stell; Chapter 1 was prepared by Gordon Maxwell and Graham Ritchie, and further contributions and advice have been provided by Catrina Appleby, Kitty Cruft, Graham Douglas, Ian Fisher, Ian Gow, Miles Oglethorpe and Ian Scott. Photographic work was undertaken by the staff of the Photographic Section (R M Adam, J D Keggie, A G Lamb, J M Mackie, A Martin, G B Quick, S Wallace); graphic work was undertaken by the staff of the Drawing Office (J Blair, J Borland, H Graham, K H MacLeod, I G Parker, I G Scott, S Scott, J N Stevenson, A Wardell).

For help received, grateful thanks are due to the following: G McGillivray (for access to Dean of Guild records and background information); Dr D Mays (for access to SOEnD draft re-survey lists, relevant particularly to 'The Clep', Court Street, and Law Hill Memorial); H Richardson (for information on hospitals and asylums); D Spence (for access to D C Thomson photographic library); Dr D M Walker (for historical recollections of recording activity in the 1950s, and for comments on draft text); and M Watson (for background information and visits to buildings of interest).

Copyright and reproduction rights held by organisations or individuals are indicated in the captions to the illustrations. All other illustrations are

View of Fernhall, West Ferry, by D M Walker (from *Nineteenth Century Mansions in the Dundee Area* **(1958)**
This remarkable volume of lithographs captures the 'jute palaces' of Dundee in a state of decay and, in many cases, collapse. Here Fernhall, built by John Sharp in 1866 to the Gothic designs of Andrew Heiton, is pictured as a gutted ruin prior to its demolition in the mid 1930s; this lithograph was drawn from an interwar photograph (NMRS B41615. Permission to reproduce: Dr D M Walker).

INTRODUCTION:
RECORDING DUNDEE'S HERITAGE

For more than 50 years after its foundation in 1908, the Royal Commission on the Ancient and Historical Monuments of Scotland was mainly confined to the preparation of records of buildings and monuments on a county-by-county basis. Counties selected for systematic survey of this kind did not include Angus; the Commission was at first only involved with Dundee in an occasional advisory capacity. In 1910, for instance, two Commissioners, Thomas Ross and W T Oldrieve, prepared a report on a proposal to add a crown to St Mary's Tower, and, in 1930, a brief descriptive and photographic record of 'Strathmartine's Lodging' was made prior to the demolition of the building.

The story of nationally-based recording of buildings in and around the city really begins in 1941, with the foundation of the Scottish National Buildings Record, for which RCAHMS assumed responsibility in 1966. The wartime origins of the SNBR are described in the Commission's publication *National Monuments Record of Scotland Jubilee; a Guide to the Collections* (1991). During the 1950s, under its Director, Colin McWilliam, SNBR's recording work began gradually to include Dundee buildings, particularly those under threat. Its photographic

surveys and acquisitions of drawings also included Dundee in, for instance, the *Vitruvius Scoticus* volume, acquired in 1945, the William Burn drawings collection, received from the RIBA in the early 1950s, and measured surveys carried out by students, such as the drawings of grave-slabs in The Howff and of the villa, 'The Vine'.

Prominent in the high level of SNBR activity in the city from the early 1950s onwards was David M Walker, the Dundee-born architectural historian. Having researched the work of local architects of the 19th and early 20th centuries when a student at Dundee College of Art, in 1953, at weekends and during vacations, Walker began recording threatened buildings in the city itself on behalf of the SNBR; he was duly supplied with a camera (an early Minolta, made of brown bakelite) and a stock of films. His 35mm photographs and others taken for the SNBR provide a poignant record of the city's surviving 'jute palaces' at a time when most were falling into a state of disrepair and collapse. Later in the decade, he made a more elaborate and stylish record of Dundee's larger houses (including those later demolished) in a volume of lithographs produced under the auspices of the College of Art. Notable among his many other drawings of the city's buildings were the aerial perspectives of jute mills prepared for a Low and Bonar company booklet, and reconstruction perspectives of major buildings, such as Dudhope Castle and the Royal Lunatic Asylum.

During the early 1960s the SNBR acquired professional photographers for the first time, thus permitting the scope of its recording work to be significantly extended into, for instance, industrial buildings and machinery under threat (such as Ward Mills and the steam engine at Clepington Waste Works).

After 1966, when the SNBR (renamed the National Monuments Record of Scotland) became part of RCAHMS, a further expansion of recording and collecting activities impinged upon Dundee. A treasure trove of historical architectural drawings of Dundee buildings was built up, acquired either directly or deposited by other institutions, especially by the Royal Incorporation of Architects in Scotland. Drawings relating to Dundee encompassed the work of illustrious national architects, such as William Burn, Frederick T Pilkington and Sir G G Scott, and of prominent local men such as David Neave (whose volume of record drawings forms part of the RIAS collection deposited in NMRS). Of special interest is a partial set of duplicate Dean of Guild plans, dating largely from the 1870s and 1880s: these provide a 'snapshot' of Dundee's evolution in the late 19th century, embracing the grandiose (such as large churches, or the Improvement Act central rebuilding schemes) and the humble (such as working-class tenements or minor alterations to jute mills). The work of local architects such as J Murray Robertson or C and L Ower is particularly well represented in this collection.

Collections of old photographs were also acquired. Subjects range from albums of late 19th-century street views to an almost complete set of views of railway stations before the Beeching closures (the Rokeby Collection) and an album of completed works by the firm of Dundee architects, Thoms and Wilkie. Also of interest, although concerning few buildings in the city itself, is a volume of photographs prepared by Charles Brand, the Dundee demolition contractor, depicting, among other things, country houses being blown up with dynamite.

The years after 1966 also saw further substantial growth in survey activity. The NMRS's own photographic survey of Private Collections was expanded: material copied included an especially valuable group of drawings of Camperdown Works in the possession of Sidlaw Industries.

The Town and Country Planning (Scotland) Acts of 1969 and 1972 entrusted RCAHMS with the duty of recording listed buildings scheduled for demolition, whilst the recording of threatened buildings of all kinds continued at a high rate. An increasingly wide variety of recording techniques was employed, ranging from purely photographic surveys, as in the case of Pilkington's Eastern Club, to fully detailed surveys comprising photographs, measured drawings and descriptive accounts as, for instance, at 70–3 High Street and Powrie Castle.

Since 1985 this work has been greatly assisted by the transfer to RCAHMS of the Scottish Industrial Archaeology Survey, which has undertaken surveys of the city's jute and other industries, including buildings under direct threat and the operations of surviving firms. Aerial photography has also made an increasing contribution to many aspects of recording activity and is especially appropriate for subjects such as extensive housing schemes, large hospitals, or football stadia. In addition, as part of a District-by-District programme intended to record prominent buildings throughout Scotland, the City of Dundee was selected for survey in 1989, and a wide range of architecture was systematically photographed. Particular emphasis was given to city centre streets, with their variety of buildings and shop-fronts, always liable to alteration, and to 20th-century suburban Dundee, where many council housing schemes and other significant buildings remain unrecorded and, for the time being, in original condition.

The NMRS records also contain a wealth of archaeological material relating to sites in City of Dundee District. Some of the earliest items belong to the extensive collection of drawings and photographs that was amassed by the Society of Antiquaries of Scotland and deposited in the Record in 1975. Dundee has yet to be the subject of intensive topographical field-survey by the Commission's officers, but several of its more conspicous monuments were recorded during the Survey of Marginal Lands in 1957. Since 1976, however, the Commission has carried out a programme of prospective aerial reconnaissance in Scotland. Though originally, and still essentially, designed to identify hitherto unrecorded sites that might be at risk from a wide spectrum of development, this form of survey also serves an invaluable strategic purpose. Overflying many areas of southern and eastern Scotland, the Commission's aerial photographic teams have gathered a heterogeneous body of information which will, over the years, gradually be assimilated into archaeological understanding.

Already, however, it has made some outstanding contributions to the study of several periods of the past, and, as will be seen in this book, Dundee has clearly been one of the beneficiaries.

Graveslab, St Mary's Tower (1991)
The most elaborate of a group of mediaeval graveslabs found when the site for the East Church was cleared in 1842. The cross is treated as a 'Tree of Life', with foliage of 13th-century type. It rises above a ship (with rudder shown in detail), which contains a soul in prayer, and a figure whose hand is raised in blessing. The status of the person commemorated is shown by the hand grasping the hilt of a sword, although the ship may indicate a merchant (NMRS B19376).

Various handwritten labels within the sketch: *Schoolhouse Longforgan*, *Castle Road, Huntly Cottage.*, *Manse*, *Gates Castle Huntly*, *Dron Chapel.*, *Dron*, *Castle Huntly*, *Mylnfield Lodge*, *Manse of Invergowrie*, *LONGFORGAN*

Composite sketch drawing of various buildings in Longforgan parish by D M Walker

Dr Walker and W M Jack recorded buildings in Tayside and Grampian rural parishes when compiling Lists of Buildings of Architectural and Historic Interest for the former Scottish Development Department in the 1960s. Walker's drawing talents were used to facilitate the process of rapid survey (NMRS printroom sketchbooks: MS/271/1, sheet 105; PTD/237/1. Permission to reproduce: Dr D M Walker).

1

EARLY DUNDEE

Most of this volume is dedicated to celebrating the last eight centuries of urban development in the City of Dundee, but the earlier stages of human settlement within the boundaries of the modern District may also be evoked pictorially. The surviving remains of such early settlement are naturally fragmentary, but archaeological discoveries made within the District over the past century have revealed traces of many stages of man's activities, while the programme of aerial photography by RCAHMS has resulted in the identification of many new sites visible only as cropmarks on air photographs.

Evidence for the earliest human activity in the Dundee area consists of a number of shell-middens and flint scatters, the traces of food-gathering and primitive tool-making practised by hunting- and fishing-communities eking out a precarious living on the shores of the River Tay more than eight thousand years ago. At Stannergate, between the Firth and the railway, traces of a flint-knapping site were found in 1878, associated with a midden containing cockles, mussels and limpets, as well as red deer antler. Flint objects were also found at Camphill, Broughty Ferry, about a decade later, but

the finds are now lost. The rich natural resources of the shores of the Tay made the estuary an obvious focus for such early settlement, and doubtless many contemporary sites have been concealed beneath urban development or later estuarine deposits.

The communities of the succeeding phase of development—the first agriculturalists—have left sparse traces of the alterations they made to the landscape from the middle of the fourth millennium BC, but the discovery of many stone axes from the District underlines the importance of woodland-felling to clear land for the fields of the first farms, and to produce timber for houses, barns and ritual monuments. It is to this period that the earliest structures represented here may possibly belong. The rectilinear ditched enclosure at Wynton, which has been revealed by air survey, has been interpreted as the remains of a long mortuary enclosure—the venue for a funerary ritual of a kind practised almost 5000 years before the present day. Comparable monuments elsewhere in Scotland (e.g. at Inchtuthil, Tayside) have been found on excavation to enclose or contain timber structures in the form of palisades or fences, where local communities might have housed their dead prior to final disposal. Such sites would have acquired considerable significance as a focus for ceremonial and funerary activity over a relatively wide area, and, in time, other structures might reasonably be expected to have sprung up in the neighbourhood. The process is exemplified at Balfarg in Fife, where possible mortuary enclosures may have been the original nucleus of a ritual complex eventually embracing a henge, cairns and a stone circle, and continuing in use until late in the second millennium BC.

About 1.2km to the NNE of Wynton lies the stone circle of Balluderon, and some 3km to the WSW aerial survey has revealed a possible henge at Dronley Wood. Although more dispersed than the complexes at Balfarg and at Forteviot on the River Earn, this grouping may usefully be compared with others in Tayside, for example the stone setting and ritual sites between Guildtown and Scone; such groupings point to a degree of concerted 'civil engineering', which might not otherwise have been expected at this early period. The handsome cup-and-ring marking on a boulder re-used in the foundations of the souterrain at Tealing provides another glimpse into the ritual practices of that time, as well as the considerable skills of contemporary craftsmen. The acquisition of metal-working technology, which occurred some time around 2500 BC, gave a wide field for the deployment of such skills. In Dundee the finely-worked gold discs from Barnhill are notable examples of such creativity; these were found in 1886, together with the blade of a bronze dagger, in a cist burial lying just outside the perimeter of a cairn. The Barnhill cist lay in a small cemetery dating to the 2nd millennium BC, by which time social trends had apparently made individual interment the custom; doubtless, funerary customs reflected a greater emphasis on individual

status in life, as well as the acquisition of personal wealth and the centralisation of secular power.

The construction of massive hilltop fortifications from the middle of the first millennium BC may be thought to demonstrate a continuation of this trend in society. One prominent example lies at the very centre of the District, crowning the summit of Dundee Law. Little is known, and less can now be seen, of the defended settlement which once looked south over the Firth, but the summits of many of the hills which stand in a protective arc round Dundee are similarly fortified, The only example to have been excavated in recent times, Hurly Hawkin in Liff and Benvie parish, was found to have a relatively complicated history of development: a promontory defended by double ditches and a rampart was subsequently used for the building of a broch, itself succeeded by a souterrain, which was constructed in the inner ditch of the earlier fort.

Similar complexity can be inferred or presumed from the available record of several other sites. At both Craighill and Laws of Monifieth a broch, exemplifying the architecture of the Atlantic Province, stands within the defences of the earlier multivallate fort. Doubtless in these cases the larger hilltop sites had long lain abandoned when, in the 1st century AD, such exotic structures were built. The nature of the changes which had overtaken a society which no longer had any use for extensive defended strongholds can only be guessed, but we need not believe that these significantly altered the way of life of the bulk of the contemporary population. It is only in the past decade that aerial survey has begun to detect in great numbers the scattered villages and hamlets of unenclosed round houses in which they lived; several hundred have now been identified in eastern Scotland north of the Forth, and they are found in particularly dense distribution in the coastal regions from the Carse of Gowrie to beyond Montrose; around Dundee there are at least a score. The individual houses were mainly of timber, and in some, much of the interior was occupied by a penannular sunken area (as reconstructed at the McManus Gallery); others are distinguished solely by an encircling ditch or gully.

Many of these settlements were associated with elongated underground structures, known as souterrains, lying adjacent to, or connecting with, individual houses. Their original purpose remains uncertain, but by the 1st century BC they appear to have been used for storage. By then they were no longer simple timber-revetted features, but elaborate, boulder-faced subterranean passages with corbelled walls and roofs formed by massive stone lintels or equally elaborate timber superstructure. Again, it has been recent aerial survey that has been most successful in their discovery; a dozen or so, like the example at Bullionfield, have come to light in the area.

The successive Roman campaigns in Scotland between the late 1st and early 3rd centuries AD probably left as little mark on such local communities as they have left on the archaeological record. The marching-camp at Longforgan merely signposts the route followed by the army of Septimius Severus in AD 208–11, while the much smaller camp at Gagie to the NE of the City has yet to be closely dated. The unexpected discovery from the air of a third temporary work at Invergowrie is thus an exciting addition to the known Roman monuments of the District.

Aerial survey has also lain behind the discovery that certain types of unenclosed settlement may have been occupied by the people we know as the Picts. Such settlements as Mylnefield appear on air photographs as subrectangular cropmarkings, which indicate sunken floors, possibly the boulder-revetted basements of robust timber buildings. Excavation of similar sites in Fife has suggested that construction techniques employed in these houses are directly descended from those of the souterrain-builders; it is thus not impossible that such settlements represent in physical form the link between the Iron Age and the communities of Dundee's Early History. With the identification of these, and their probable contemporaries, the cemeteries of small square and circular barrows at Star Inn Farm, the catalogue of archaeological evidence of Dundee's past from primitive state to pre-urban settlement is made inestimably richer.

Some of these settlements and burials probably belonged to communities who had newly received the message of Christianity. Other groups of burials in slab-lined graves or 'long cists', of a type common among the Christian Britons of south-east Scotland, were discovered at Stannergate in the 18th and 19th centuries. However, in the Dundee area as elsewhere in Pictland, our knowledge of religious activity, artistic patronage and cultural links in the period between the 7th and 12th centuries is derived mainly from carved stones. The enigmatic animal and geometrical symbols peculiar to the Pictish area are found on three undressed slabs with incised symbols (Linlathen, Strathmartine, Longforgan); on a number of complete or fragmentary slabs carved in relief with ornamented crosses (Balluderon, Monifieth, Murroes, Strathmartine, Tealing); and on the unique crescent-shaped bronze plaque, now lost, from Laws of Monifieth.

The fashion for riders, human figures and interlaced animals, as displayed on the cross-slabs, continued in the period after the middle of the 9th century, when the Picts were united with the Scots of Dalriada (Argyll) in the new kingdom of Scotland and the symbols ceased to be used. New artistic influences from Ireland and Northumbria are also found, and new types of monument included free-standing crosses at Monifieth and Strathmartine and a recumbent grave-cover at Strathmartine. These two sites are notable for groups of monuments indicating religious observance over long periods, while the continuing importance of the area immediately west of the present city is marked by the late cross-slabs from Benvie and Invergowrie, and the unique 'portrait' slab of a horseman drinking from a bird-headed horn, found in 1934 during the construction of the city by-pass at Bullion.

Wynton, Mains and Strathmartine (1982)
Cropmarks on an aerial photograph show a rectangular structure, possibly of ritual character and dating to the third millennium BC. The cropmarks between the enclosure and the public road are difficult to interpret, but they may be traces of a round barrow cemetery (NMRS AN/5922).

Dronley Wood, Auchterhouse (1984)
Revealed on this aerial photograph as a cropmark in a field of ripening barley, there is a roughly circular enclosure, possibly a henge monument; if this interpretation is correct, the enclosure belongs to a class of site, often provided with uprights in timber or stone, used for communal ceremonies in the third millennium BC (NMRS A64781).

Laws of Monifieth, Fort and Broch

On the summit of the hill are the remains of a massively-built stone-walled fort and broch which were extensively explored in the course of excavations in 1859.

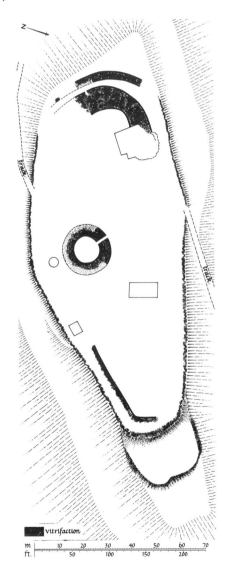

vitrifaction

Watercolour of the broch prepared in 1859 (Society of Antiquaries of Scotland Collection, NMRS DC14985).

Plan prepared as part of RCAHMS Marginal Land survey in 1957 (NMRS AND/1/3).

Burnhead of Auchterhouse, Souterrain (1984)
Aerial photography has nearly doubled the number of
souterrains revealed around Dundee; this dramatic view
shows the curving walls of the souterrain picked out as a
light coloured cropmarking in a field of barley (NMRS
A64155).

Auchray, Fort (1984)
This fort overlooked Clatto Reservoir from the north, and,
although little can now be seen on the ground, cropmarks on
aerial photographs reveal that it was originally defended by at
least five lines of ditches (NMRS A64777).

Tealing, Cup-and-ring Marked Stone (1985)
This massive boulder, incorporated in the wall of the souterrain (see below), is decorated with distinctive cup-markings and cup-and-ring markings belonging to the third or second millennium BC   (NMRS A35489).

Tealing, Souterrain
The souterrain at Tealing which was discovered in the course of agriculture operations in 1871 is a classic example of this class of monument, with curving underground passage and corbelled side-walls.

Ground view showing the massive boulders at the base of the side-walls (1986)   (NMRS A35017).

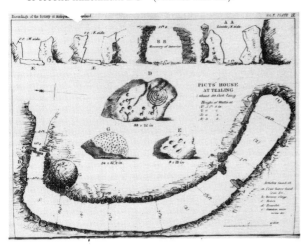

Plan illustrating the original discovery as reported in the *Proceedings of the Society of Antiquaries of Scotland* (NMRS DC14988/po).

Longforgan, Roman Marching-camp (1983)
Straddling a prominent ridge a little to the north-west of Longforgan, this marching-camp is represented by the cropmark of the enclosing ditch, the accompanying rampart having long since been destroyed by cultivation. The rounded north-west angle of the camp and portions of the adjacent sides are clearly visible   (NMRS PT/14405).

Mylnefield, Unenclosed Settlement (1986)
To the east of Mylnefield House cropmark traces of what
may be a group of subrectangular sunken-floored houses are
visible on this aerial view (NMRS A30760).

**Laws of Monifieth, crescent-shaped bronze plaque
(1880)**
This engraving reproduces a drawing made in 1796 when
this unique plaque was found in a burial-mound near the
fort and broch on the Laws of Monifieth. Decorated with
Pictish symbols the plaque, now lost, also bears a Norse
runic inscription, *[Gri]mkitil,* dating to about the eleventh
century.

Invergowrie, cross-slab
This cross-slab, dating to the middle of the ninth century,
bears a ringed cross on one face and, on the back, three
clerics, each holding a book and two of them wearing cloaks
with what may be cross-marked brooches at the shoulders.
Below are two symmetrical dragons. The slab is now in the
Royal Museum of Scotland (NMRS AN/35).

2

MEDIAEVAL AND POST-MEDIAEVAL DUNDEE

The centre of present-day Dundee, the area occupied by the mediaeval burgh, retains only one significant building of mediaeval date: the 15th-century tower of the Parish Church of St Mary, which when complete was one of the largest burgh churches in mediaeval Scotland and was subdivided into four congregations after the Reformation. Surviving remains even from the 17th and 18th centuries are now, however, scarce, while the early shoreline has been obscured by continuous land reclamation since the 17th century.

Centred around Seagate, the first settlement was elevated by Earl David of Huntingdon to the status of a burgh in about 1191. The following century witnessed rapid growth, especially to the west, with buildings clustered around the castle (now vanished) and the church of St Clement, which stood approximately on the site of City Square; the harbour was located immediately to the south. The town's first tolbooth was built after 1325 in Seagate. During the later Middle Ages Dundee, with its large agricultural hinterland and eastward-facing estuary, emerged as a strong centre of northern European trade. Its street-plan was increasingly centred around Marketgate (present-day High Street), where a

second tolbooth was located, and from which led the principal streets: Nethergate (to the west), Overgate (to the north-east), Seagate (to the east) and Murraygate (to the north-east). These streets were lined with timber-framed buildings, generally comprising the larger merchants' houses on the main frontages with working premises and humbler dwellings in the backlands. Probably the largest timber-fronted 15th-century house, Our Lady Warkstairs, was demolished in 1879.

By 1600, Dundee was the second largest burgh in the country, with a diversified economy in which textile manufacture was already strongly represented. This prosperity increasingly made possible, during the 16th, 17th and early 18th centuries, construction of merchants' houses in stone (with crowstepped gables) as in the case of Gardyne's House (*c*.1600) at the rear of 70–3 High Street, or the now-demolished Strathmartine's Lodging (which was situated to the rear of St Clement's Church). The wealth of Dundee's burgesses was also reflected in the increasingly elaborate monuments erected in the town's burial-ground, The Howff. The town walls, also a measure of prosperity as well as need, were built only at the end of the 16th century. Outside the walls, in the immediate hinterland of the burgh, the relative peace that followed the Reformation and earlier English incursions also permitted, in the late 16th century, the building or enlargement of substantial fortified residences, such as Dudhope, Claypotts and Mains Castles.

This period of prosperity came to an abrupt end, however, in the middle of the 17th century. The Civil War brought devastation to the town, which was plundered in Montrose's raid of 1645 and Monck's of 1651. Throughout the remainder of the 17th and early 18th centuries, Dundee's economy stagnated, and its population remained at or below 10,000.

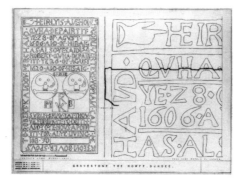

The Howff; drawing of gravestone by W F Howitt (c. 1955)
In 1564, the Greyfriars gardens and orchards were granted to the town by Queen Mary as a cemetery, owing to the inadequacy of St Clement's churchyard. Between that date and the 1830s, the Howff was Dundee's principal burial-ground, and many elaborate funerary monuments were erected, some particularly good examples dating from the 17th century. The cemetery's name derived from the fact that, until the completion of the Trades Hall in 1776, it served as a meeting place for the Nine Trades. The Howff ceased to be used for burials in 1878 (NMRS AND/65, B41629. Permission to reproduce: Dundee School of Architecture).

St Mary's Church and Tower; view by R W Billings
The original mediaeval church was much damaged by English attacks from the mid 16th century onwards, and was destroyed by fire in 1841 with the exception of the late 15th-century tower—at 156 feet (47m) in height, the highest surviving mediaeval ecclesiastical tower in Scotland—and the Steeple Church, built in 1789. Following the 1841 fire, the Town's Churches were rebuilt to the designs of William Burn. R W Billings's volumes, *The Baronial and Ecclesiastical Antiquities of Scotland* (1845–52), constituted the first serious antiquarian record of Scottish mediaeval buildings. This view portrays the tower prior to Sir George Gilbert Scott's restoration of 1872 (NMRS AND/85/1).

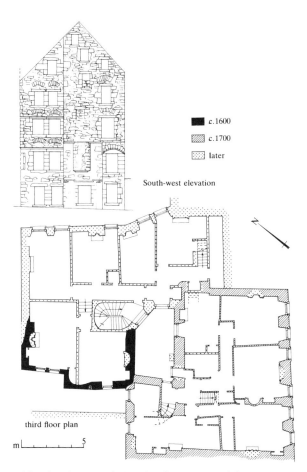

c.1600
c.1700
later

South-west elevation

third floor plan

m _____ 5

'Gardyne's House', Gray's Close, 70–3 High Street; elevation to Gray's Close and third-floor plan (surveyed 1976)

This five-storeyed block, erected in the late 16th century, is the last survivor of Dundee's stone-built post-mediaeval merchant's houses. It forms part of a group of three buildings set around a courtyard on the north side of the High Street: the front block is an 18th-century tenement.

Our Lady Warkstairs, Church Lane (c. 1870)

The largest timber-fronted 15th-century house in Dundee, seen before its demolition in 1879 during Improvement Act clearances (NMRS B41658).

11

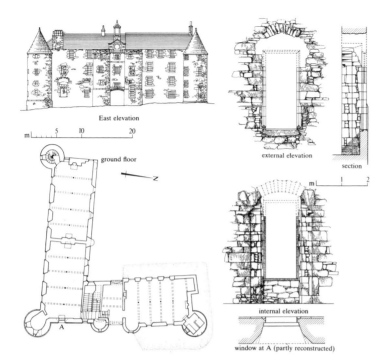

East elevation

ground floor

external elevation

section

internal elevation

window at A (partly reconstructed)

Dudhope Castle

A late mediaeval tower house, seat of the Scrymgeour family, Constables of Dundee, was extended after 1580 to form a massive L-plan structure with circular angle towers: the tower was later demolished, and the building was converted to a woollen mill and barracks in the 18th century. In 1958, following a period of Ministry of Works occupation, the Corporation made an abortive attempt to demolish the castle; it was eventually restored in 1985–8.

East elevation, ground-floor plan and window details (surveyed 1986).

Reconstruction drawing by D M Walker (1958)

The roofs are here restored to their 17th-century profile, but the 1799 clock gable and bell turret are retained; indicated floor-levels on the south front are conjectural (NMRS B41655. Permission to reproduce: Dr D M Walker).

Mains Castle

This fortified house, constructed in 1562–80 as the seat of the Grahams of Fintry, was acquired in 1913 by the Town Council and eventually restored in the 1980s (NMRS AND/147, B41630. Permission to reproduce: Dr D M Walker).

North elevation by D M Walker with sketched reconstruction details (1961) (NMRS AND/147, B41630. Permission to reproduce: Dr D M Walker).

NORTH FRONT

View by Valentine of Dundee (1878)
(NMRS AN/2195, B41656).

13

Claypotts Castle; drawing by Waller Hugh Paton (1861)

An archetypal Z-plan castle, built between 1569 and 1588 for John Strachan. Following a period in derelict condition, it was placed in Ministry of Works guardianship in 1926 and subsequently restored. Paton, an antiquarian artist, sketched numerous castles, churches and stones (NMRS B41642).

3

GEORGIAN DUNDEE

Dundee recovered only slowly from the ravages of the 17th century. But, encouraged by the introduction of bounties on exported linen in 1742, a prosperous coarse linen manufacturing and exporting trade began to emerge, and the town's population rose from 12,000 in 1750 to nearly 27,000 in 1800 and to over 60,000 in 1840. Increasingly, the wealthy merchants left the centre for suburban houses, and the undeveloped backlands were filled by industrial structures. As the linen trade boomed, annual outward tonnage rose from 3,500 in 1745 to 21,331 in 1791, and the harbour became increasingly inadequate. In 1815, the Dundee Harbour Commissioners engaged Thomas Telford to draw up enlargement plans, and in 1830 an Act of Parliament created the Dundee Harbour Trust.

During the 18th century, the gradual remodelling of the centre began: new streets such as Crichton Street were laid out, and substantial classical public buildings were erected, most notably William Adam's Town House (1732–4) and Samuel Bell's St Andrew's Church (1772). However, in contrast to some other major urban centres such as Edinburgh, there was no attempt to undertake comprehensive remodelling or construction of classically-planned town extensions. Even the passing of an Improvement Act in 1825 resulted only in piecemeal replanning. One formal new artery, Reform Street, was laid out, terminated axially by the portico of George Angus's Public Seminaries (1832–4).

As the wealthy merchants forsook the centre, so Dundee's suburbs rapidly expanded; all but one of the town gates were removed by about 1770. Suburban growth was most vigorous in the north and north-west, and in isolated cases such as South Tay Street this took the form of terraces. But, from the early 19th century, villas soon established predominance in areas such as Chapelshade, Dudhope and Magdalen Yard; at the other end of the town, villas also proliferated in West Ferry and Broughty Ferry. On an altogether larger scale, 1824–6 saw the construction (for the 1st Earl of Camperdown) of Camperdown House, a country mansion to the north-west of Dundee, broadly based on the design of Grange Park, Hampshire. The edge of the town also naturally attracted large new institutions, such as Stark's Royal Asylum (begun 1812).

Many prominent buildings, especially after c.1820,

were designed by architects whose practices were based outside Dundee; not only did William Burn himself work in the town, but his assistants, George Smith and George Angus, also established themselves there. This period also saw the emergence of local designers of some calibre. Most prominent were the two Town's Architects of the late 18th and early 19th centuries, Samuel Bell (designer of the Trades Hall, Episcopal Chapel and St Andrew's Church) and David Neave (Town's Architect 1813–33, and designer of numerous villas of refined classical detail). Their position, and some aspects of their work (such as Neave's design for South Tay Street), presaged the municipal architecture of the later 19th and 20th centuries. During this period a close and sometimes controversial inter-relation between Dundee's municipal and business interests was established, most particularly by the activities of Provost Alexander Riddoch, an associate of Neave.

High Street
View from west (c. 1878)
This view shows, on the right, the classical Town House designed in 1731 by William Adam and built in 1732–4 to replace the old Tolbooth, and in the left distance the elegant Trades Hall (designed in 1776 by Samuel Bell); the mid 19th-century spire of St. Paul's Episcopal Cathedral is at centre. Other 18th-century buildings are also visible (NMRS B41669; album 67).

Design for Town House by William Adam, *Vitruvius Scoticus* **(published** *c.* **1812), plate 104; north elevation and plan**
The building, affectionately known as 'The Pillars', contained a vaulted ground-floor arcade with shops and bank; above were council chambers, courts and jail (NMRS AND/159/1).

ST. ANDREW'S KIRK
and Glasite Meeting House.

View of St Andrew's Church and Glasite Church; lithograph drawn by D M Walker (1960)
St Andrew's Church, designed by Samuel Bell, was built in 1772 and the octagonal Glasite Church in 1777. At St Andrew's, Bell made his debut as the first Town's Architect, probably with the assistance of plans prepared by James Craig (NMRS B40999. Permission to reproduce: Dr D M Walker).

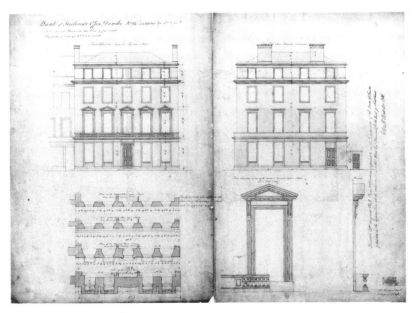

Reform Street

Dundee's only equivalent to the classical city-centre developments of Edinburgh, Glasgow and Aberdeen was projected in 1824 by William Burn and opened in 1833. Plots were feued from 1834, and were developed throughout the mid-19th century.

Design by William Burn for proposed Bank of Scotland, 34 Reform Street (1842) (NMRS AND/38).

Perspective of proposed alterations to 34 Reform Street by George Shaw Aitken (1880)
A later Victorian remodelling of Burn's building (NMRS B41625; RIAS Drawings Collection).

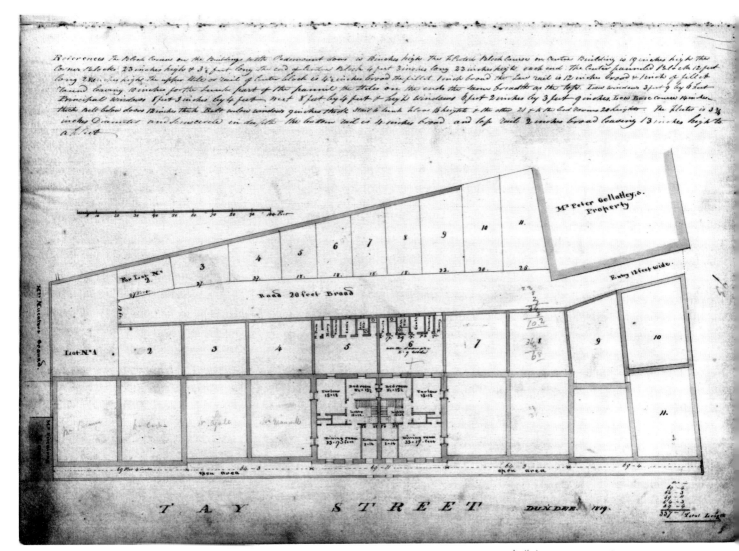

South Tay Street; plan of the different lots (1819), contained in David Neave volume of architectural drawings

One of Dundee's few Georgian terraces of dwellings, laid out through hospital gardens in 1792–3 as building plots for merchants. The south terrace (nos 1–27) was built in 1818–29 to the designs of David Neave, who occupied one of the houses himself (NMRS B41652; RIAS Drawings Collection).

Dundee High School

The High School, which provides an axial termination to Reform Street, was built in 1832–4 to the Greek Doric designs of George Angus. Orginally known as the Dundee Public Seminaries, it at first housed the Academy, the Grammar School and the English School. It was substantially extended in the late 19th century and again after 1945.

View of south façade by Colin McWilliam (1956)
(NMRS AN/1739/8, 9).

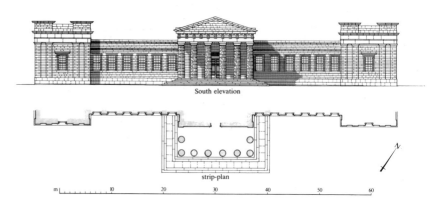

South elevation

strip-plan

Elevation and plan of south façade (1991)

20

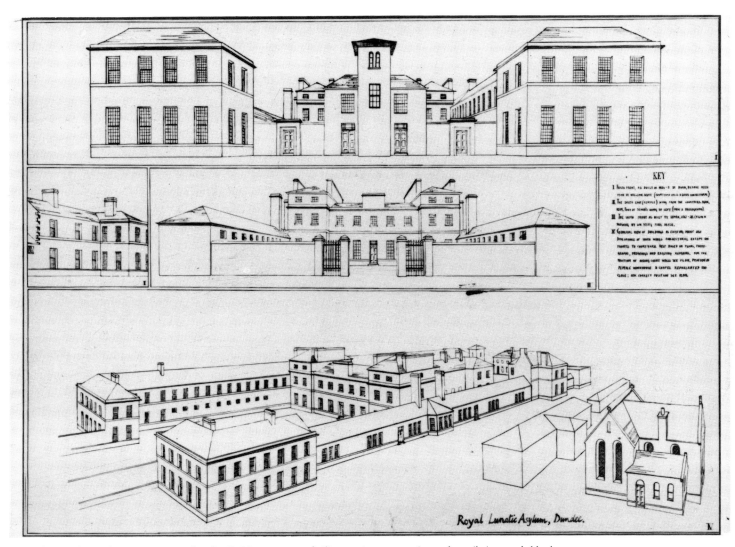

Royal Lunatic Asylum, Dundee.

Royal Lunatic Asylum; reconstruction by D M Walker, showing Asylum as built in four stages from 1812 to 1860 (1952)

Built in 1812–20 to the designs of William Stark, a versatile architect. Here, Stark moved away from the radial plan of his earlier asylum at Glasgow, and adopted an 'H'-layout, housing the inmates in single-storeyed wings intended to facilitate patient segregation and ventilation, probably the first example of such a layout in Scotland. Stark claimed that this was a system 'which every asylum ought especially to keep in view, that of great gentleness and great liberty and comfort combined with the fullest security'. The building was extended by William Burn, whose designs were based on an asylum at Wakefield (NMRS AND/6/11, 2; B20949).

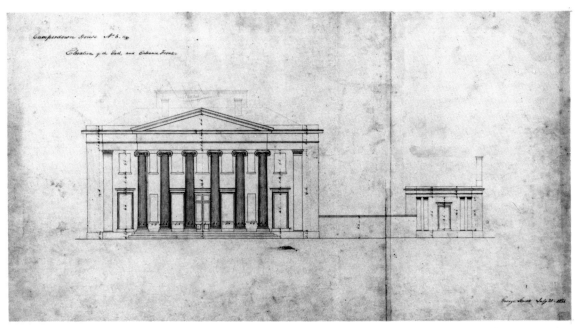

Camperdown House; design by William Burn for entrance elevation (1821)

An exceptional Greek Revival country house designed by William Burn in 1821 for the 2nd Viscount Duncan (created 1st Earl of Camperdown); its name commemorated the famous victory won by Viscount Duncan's father, Admiral Lord Duncan, at the Battle of Camperdown in 1797 (NMRS AND/48/6. Permission to reproduce: Lt Col M H Warriner).

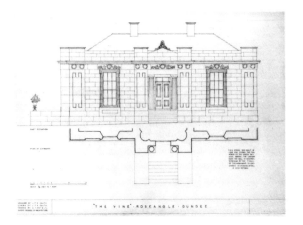

'The Vine', 43 Magdalen Yard Road; east elevation and plan of east façade; record drawing by J F K Smith (1955)

A single-storeyed Graeco-Egyptian villa, built as an art gallery and house for George Duncan, MP, in 1836; architect not known (NMRS AND/80, B41627).

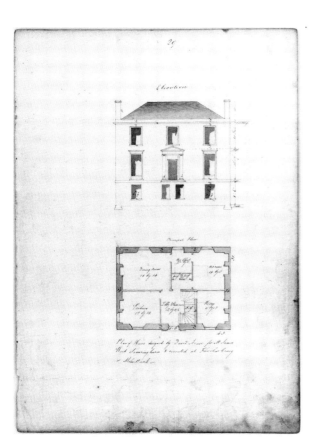

24 Milnbank Road; north elevation and plan, from David Neave volume of architectural drawings (c. 1815)
A small house built *c.* 1815 for James Reid to the classical designs of David Neave: one of the architect's most competent Dundee villas. Gutted 1986 (NMRS B41653; RIAS Drawings Collection).

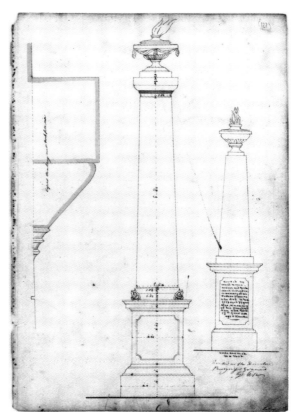

Neave volume of architectural drawings; designs for two monuments (c. 1813) (NMRS B41648; RIAS Drawings Collection).

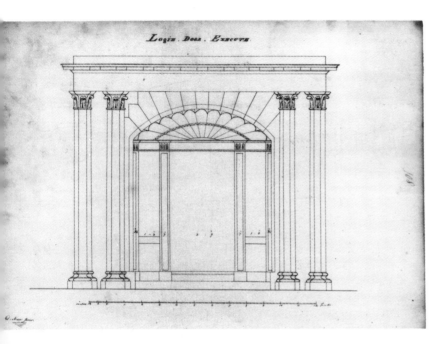

Logie House
A villa built *c.* 1813 for Isaac Watt and designed by David Neave; now demolished.

Elevation of main door, contained in David Neave volume of architectural drawings (*c.* 1813) (NMRS B41649; RIAS Drawings Collection).

View of main façade by David Walker (from *Nineteenth Century Mansions* **(1958))** (NMRS B41613. Permission to reproduce: Dr D M Walker).

4

VICTORIAN AND EDWARDIAN DUNDEE

The chief force behind Dundee's 19th-century growth was the town's sudden industrial development, above all in jute processing and manufacture. Following the abandonment of the jute bounty (an export subsidy) in 1832, the response of the town's jute merchants was to go 'down-market'. They began to concentrate on the import of cheap fibres and the manufacture of coarse jute cloth, which was needed in prodigious quantities as world trade expanded, especially for the making of sacks. A small amount of jute was spun in 1832, and a manufacturing boom soon followed. The decisive impetus, however, came from the successive demands of the Crimean War and the American Civil War in the 1850s and 1860s, by which time power-driven machinery was becoming ubiquitous. By 1911, textile employment accounted for 48% of total employment in the city and 69% of female employment: high female employment and low wages were to remain the characteristics of this industry.

The building of jute mills closely followed the cyclical peaks in manufacturing activity, in 1833–6, 1864–7, and 1871–4; however, the largest firms were also able to expand during the leaner years between.

Mills were concentrated along two watercourses, the Scouringburn to the north-west and the Dens Burn to the north-east, with a detached north-western group in Lochee. Initially, large mills took the form of multi-storeyed stone-built structures of plain classical appearance, and, to prevent damaging losses from fire, iron-framed construction was essential. The first large fireproof mill, Logie Mill, was built from 1828 onwards. In the middle decades of the 19th century, large, high blocks proliferated, generally designed not by architects but by textile engineering companies or by the engineering departments of textile manufacturers. The most prominent examples were the large mills built by the most powerful jute dynasties: Dens Works (Baxter), Camperdown Works (Cox), Bowbridge Works (Grimond) and Tay Works (Gilroy). From the early 1870s, however, there was a complete change in mill planning. High blocks were almost completely rejected in favour of extensive single-storeyed complexes, the pioneering examples being Caldrum Works (1872) and Manhattan Works (1873). Other jute-related processes were associated with elaborate machines and structures, such as calenders (massive composite rolling machines for jute finishing), steam engines and chimney stalks, the tallest and most famous example of which was 'Cox's Stack', erected at Camperdown Works in 1865–6.

None of Dundee's other industries even remotely approached the scale of jute. Within the engineering industry, some firms, such as Robertson and Orchar, made machines for use in jute manufacturing; but there also flourished other, general mechanical and electrical engineering concerns, such as Sturrock and Murray (founded in 1914).

The town's industrial boom was fuelled by vigorous building in many other spheres. One vital area of improvement was transportation. The first railway links out of Dundee were established in the 1830s, and the first Tay Bridge was completed in 1878. Even more important, perhaps, was the continuing development of the harbour, with new docks built in the third quarter, and new wharves in the fourth quarter, of the 19th century. Some industrial activity was inevitably of a maritime character. In shipbuilding, substantial firms such as W B Thompson (later Caledon Shipbuilding) established themselves in the late 19th century. Whaling, too, assumed a brief prominence as a result of the spread of auxiliary steam power in the late 1850s and 1860s: by 1872, the town had become Britain's premier whaling port, with twelve whalers registered, but the industry in Dundee declined and finally collapsed between 1881 and 1911 as a result of over-exploitation.

To underpin industrial expansion, it was also necessary to provide large numbers of working-class dwellings within easy reach of Dundee's industrial areas. Within a few decades, the flow of immigrants from the Tayside rural hinterland, and from the Highlands and Ireland, turned Dundee into a predominantly working-class town. The unskilled poor were accommodated chiefly in subdivided older properties in the mediaeval centre, although much displacement was caused by Improvement Act redevelopments from the 1870s onwards. Skilled workers were housed chiefly in large numbers of new dwellings erected mainly in the 1840s, the 1870s and the later 1890s: between 1867 and 1914, 20,567 houses were built.

Never could it be said that Dundee lacked plentiful building land. The large-scale building of houses took place on a succession of boundary estates; the first in 1831 extended for one mile in all directions (north, east and west), whilst three others between 1859 and 1892 ranged to the west and north-west. There were no significant political obstacles to Dundee's expansion, the only possible rivals, the burghs of Lochee and Broughty Ferry, being absorbed in 1859 and 1913 respectively. Accordingly, by the late 19th century, working-class housing was spreading, largely uncontrolled, in all directions that had not been pre-empted by middle-class development, that is, to areas such as Hawkhill and Blackness Road (at the north-west), Hilltown (at the north) and Dens Road (at the north-east).

These new working-class houses were contained in tenements, of which the most typical were four-storeyed blocks with rear balcony access and stone staircase towers (often with later brick spurs containing water-closets), a pattern not found to any great extent in Scotland's other three major cities. Most Dundee tenement flats were of one or two rooms only, a category accounting for 60% of all dwellings in the city in 1918. This phenomenon is explicable partly by lower wages, but also partly by the fact that, at that time, Scottish working-class dwellings still adhered to the normal European pattern of relatively large and tall rooms (rather than the English custom of smaller, but more numerous rooms). Most working-class and middle-class houses in Dundee and elsewhere were speculatively built, although there were several instances of development by working men's associations and similar groups: the concrete dwellings in Court Street, built in 1874–5, are a case in point.

While the pace of working-class housing development accelerated, the movement of the wealthier classes away from the disease-prone centre to even further-flung suburbs continued apace. But this trend entered a new and dramatic phase after 1850 when Dundee's principal industrialists embarked on the construction of suburban homes of a most grandiose kind, seemingly in competition with each other. The first spate of building occurred in the 1850s, with the building of villas such as Clement Park, Lochee, by the Camperdown chief, James Cox. The late 1860s, however, witnessed the erection of the two most ambitious of these jute palaces on prominent sites in Broughty Ferry: George Gilroy's Castleroy, a craggy Tudor group with extensive conservatory and Gothic staircase hall, and Joseph Grimond's richly decorated extensions to Kerbat House (renamed Carbet Castle). Numerous smaller villas were built during the late 19th and early 20th centuries by Dundee's lesser manufacturers. It is now difficult to imagine oneself back in this opulent, gas-lit world, which fell into decay in the 1930s and finally vanished virtually without trace in the grey austerity years following World War II. Only a few records survive, such as the photographs of the interior of Beechwood (a second-rank Cox house) during the 1870s, preserved in the collections of the Scottish National Portrait Gallery.

To sustain the burgeoning life of the industrial town, other social provisions were vital: hospitals, such as the new Royal Infirmary; schools, such as the Morgan Hospital (1863–7, designed by Peddie and Kinnear) or the new public elementary schools built following the passing of the 1872 Education (Scotland) Act and in the early years of the 20th century; and churches, with prolific building by all denominations to the designs of local architects and national designers such as F T Pilkington or Sir G G Scott.

Given Dundee's dramatic mid-century growth, it is perhaps surprising that no attempt was made to undertake the reconstruction of the congested mediaeval core to provide a modern commercial centre. The main reason was quite simply that, owing to earlier financial problems, the Town Council was effectively bankrupt between 1842 and 1864. The city was stirred from its inactivity only after the appointment of a new and energetic Burgh Surveyor, William Mackinson, in 1868, and the passing of a further Improvement Act in 1871. Between 1871 and 1891, Mackison forced through the rebuilding of almost all of the pre-Georgian centre, commencing with Commercial Street and proceeding to such schemes as Whitehall Street and Crescent, and Victoria Road. In the process, most of the surviving mediaeval merchants' houses were demolished, and replaced by tall, relatively homogeneous Haussmannesque classical frontages erected piecemeal, but within Mackison's guidelines. Commercial building also proceeded at a rapid pace outside the Improvement Act schemes, in styles ranging from the 12th-century French Gothic of Young and Meldrum's Queen's Hotel (1878) to the Thomsonesque Greek of J Murray Robertson's India Buildings, Bell Street (1874–6).

INDUSTRY
Jute processes; spinning

The preparation and spinning into yarn of raw jute fibre involves numerous complex and inter-related processes.

Queen Victoria Works, Brook Street; drawings of spinning processes (1989)   (NMRS B20934, 5).

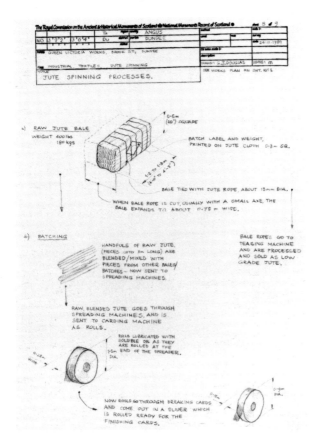

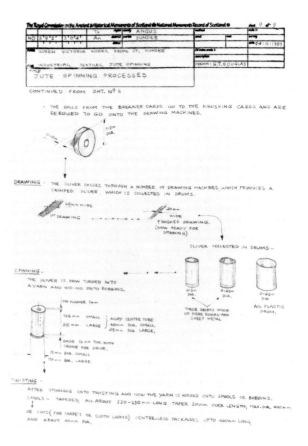

Jute processes; weaving
Up to the early 20th century, nearly all weaving and finishing machinery was made in Dundee by firms such as Urquhart Lindsay and Company, and Robertson and Orchar.

Constable Works; view of breaker card machine (1990)
Viewed here from its feed side, this machine was made by Fairbairn of Leeds (NMRS B20462).

Constable Works; Robertson and Orchar 72-inch loom in operation (1990)
This loom, which was made possibly in the early 1920s, is here seen weaving a special jute/wire mix (NMRS B20419).

Jute processes; finishing
The woven cloth is finished in calenders, which consist of massive arrays of horizontal cast-iron and compressed-paper rolls. Afterwards, it may be packed into bales by hydraulic presses, or made directly into sacking with the aid of special cutting, sewing and printing machines. Alternatively, hessian may be despatched in rolls for use in carpet and linoleum manufacture.

Constable Works; view of calender (1990)
This calender was made in 1919 by Robertson and Orchar: it was electrically driven, through V-belt pulleys, but was later converted to hydraulic operation (NMRS B20420).

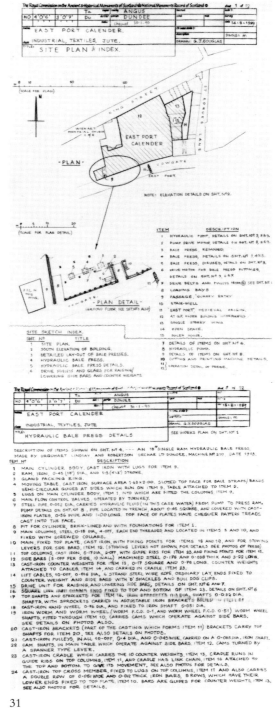

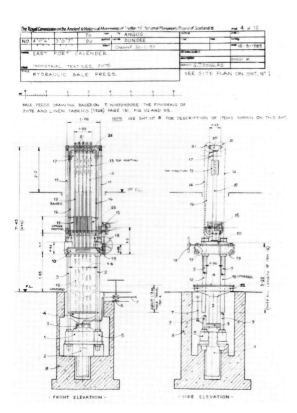

Hydraulic bale-presses, East Port Calender, Cowgate; site plan, drawing and description of central bale-press (1989)

These presses were designed by Robert Gibson, engineer, and installed by Urquhart Lindsay and Company during a reconstruction of the works in 1913. The works closed in 1989 (NMRS B20938–9, 20944).

Taybank Works, Arbroath Road; the sack–making department at work (1986)   NMRS A61437).

Jute works; steam plant

South Dudhope Jute Works (Alexander Henderson and Sons); view of tandem compound horizontal engine (1967)
This engine, made in 1899 by James Carmichael and Co., Ward Foundry, drove 154 looms and four dressing machines. It was shut down in 1966 and scrapped in 1967 (NMRS AN/624).

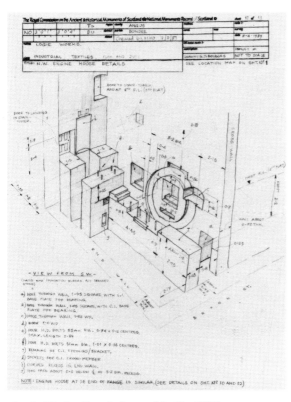

Logie Works, Brook Street ('Coffin Mill')
The original block, built 1828 and probably designed by
Umpherston and Kerr, was extended in 1833 and 1839: it
was the first iron-framed mill to be built by local engineers,
and was the largest mill in Dundee until the 1860s.

**North-west engine house; view from south-west
(1989)**
This view shows Graham Douglas inspecting the flywheel
recess and crankshaft bearing pad (NMRS B17509).

Logie Works, South-west block; view of fourth-floor flat showing brick-vaulted construction (1986) (NMRS A38413).

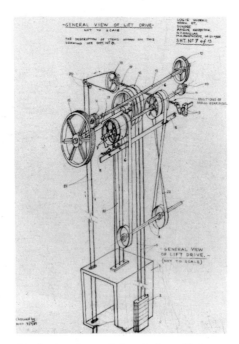

South-west block; drawing and description of belt-driven lift by Graham Douglas, 1986 (NMRS

View of wrought-iron walkway and north-east block (1986) (NMRS A38411).

Dens Works, Princes Street; aerial view drawn by D M Walker (*c.* 1953), for Low and Bonar company brochure

This factory group, established in 1822 by William Baxter, was developed and subsequently extended over a period of 130 years. The earliest extant building is Upper Dens Mill, one of Scotland's first large fire-proof mills. It was commenced in 1833 to the designs of Umpherston and Kerr, and was extended in 1850–1 by Peter Carmichael and Randolph Elliott. The group was partly redeveloped in the early 1980s (NMRS B40901. Permission to reproduce: Dr D M Walker).

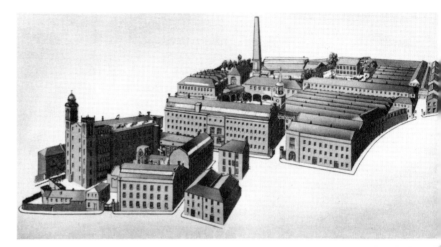

Ward Mills, North Lindsay Street; view of attic (1964)

This mill, built in 1857–72, included a tall, five-storeyed south wing with Italianate bell tower and ornate cast-iron roof. It was demolished in 1964 (NMRS AN/223).

TAY WORKS, DUNDEE.
MESSRS GILROY, SONS, & CO., LIMITED.
JUTE SPINNERS AND MANUFACTURERS.

Tay Works, Lochee Road; perspective view from east (1891)
Tay Works was established in the early 19th century by W Boyack, the city's largest flax-spinning enterprise. In 1849, seven years after Boyack's bankruptcy, it was acquired by Gilroy Brothers, who enlarged it into an extensive spinning and weaving works, creating a spectacular east frontage to Lochee Road, about 680 feet (190m) in length. The earliest parts of this frontage date from the 1830s and 1850s; it was completed in 1871 (NMRS A45526).

Camperdown Works, Methven Street

The world's largest jute works was developed here from 1850 onwards, and by the end of the century employed 5,000 people. The most prominent features of Camperdown are the High Mill, built in 1857–68 to the designs of Cox and Carmichael, and the 283 feet (86m)–high Cox's Stack, built in polychromatic brick in 1865–6 to the designs of Cox and Maclaren. The works was closed in 1981, with the exception of the Calender, and most buildings other than Cox's Stack and the High Mill were subsequently demolished.

Aerial perspective of works from south-west (late 19th century) (NMRS A45532. Permission to reproduce: Sidlaw Industries).

The same view following demolition of most buildings (1988) (NMRS A55843).

Dundee whaling industry; walrus-skinning in progress on the deck of a Dundee Arctic whaler (*c.* 1890) (Copyright: Dundee Art Galleries and Museums).

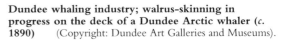
Victoria Dock, steam crane; detail of rotary drive (1973)
Already partly in use by 1848, Victoria Dock was completed under an Act of 1869. The 90-ton crane was one of the largest in the Dundee Docks (NMRS AN/2603).

Tay Bridge Station; view from north-east during construction, *c.* 1877
Tay Bridge Station, built by the North British Railway, was opened in 1878, shortly before completion of the first Tay Bridge (Copyright: D C Thomson Ltd).

First Tay Bridge; the inaugural passenger train, a directors' special, leaving the Fife end (26 September 1878)
A single-track bridge built by the North British Railway in 1871–8 to the designs of Sir Thomas Bouch; the contractors were Charles de Bergue & Co., and Hopkinson Gilkes & Co. The central girders blew down in a gale on 28 December 1879 (NMRS A38639. Permission to reproduce: Lord Palmer).

DOMESTIC ARCHITECTURE: 'JUTE PALACES' TO TENEMENTS

Castleroy, Broughty Ferry

With almost a hundred rooms, Castleroy was the largest and grandest of the 'jute palaces'. It was built in 1867 for the Gilroys of Tay Works, to the Tudor designs of the architect, Andrew Heiton. Concerning its architecture, Walker wrote: 'Although the house had a strange fascination, it was unsuccessful: the external composition was mismanaged, and cursed with the same hardness of detail as Fernhall'. During World War II, the house was requisitioned for use as a headquarters for Polish forces, and was then taken over for a time by squatters. In 1946, the trustees of the late A B Gilroy offered it as a gift to the Corporation, who used it as emergency accommodation for families on the housing waiting list. As a result of lack of maintenance, dry rot became established in the service wing. Despite efforts by the City Architect, Robert Dron, to check its further encroachment by stripping out numerous rooms, the dry rot rapidly spread to the main block. In November 1954, the house was bought by the demolition contractor, Charles Brand, and, in 1955, was razed to the ground. Over the year before its demolition, photographic records were made for the SNBR by D M Walker and by the College of Art photographer.

Photograph of mirror-backed side table on west wall of Dining Room, taken by D M Walker (1954) (NMRS B41657).

View of staircase hall, taken by D M Walker (1954)
The staircase hall's style was a harsh French Gothic, with arches supported by red granite columns. Walker's final survey, in late 1954 and early 1955, captured the melancholy atmosphere of the derelict house immediately prior to its demolition. (NMRS AN/2090/2. Permission to reproduce: Dr D M Walker).

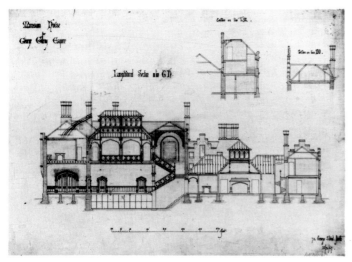

Design for Castleroy by Andrew Heiton (1867); longitudinal section (NMRS AND/42/2).

Dining Room; view of north-east corner by D M Walker (1953) (NMRS AN/2537, B20947).

Carbet Castle, Broughty Ferry

In 1861 Joseph Grimond, co-founder of Bowbridge Works, bought Kerbat House in Broughty Ferry, and extended it with richly-decorated east and west wings designed in French Renaissance style by Thomas Saunders Robertson. Demolition was already under way between way between the wars, and by the 1950s there only remained the west wing (containing a sumptuous ground-floor Dining Room and first-floor saloon, with ceilings of 1871 by the French artist Charles Frechou) and an earlier rear service block, both in semi-ruinous condition. The first records were made in 1953 by David Walker, who recalls that 'for Carbet, my camera was totally inadequate! I originally heard about it from William and Norah Montgomerie; at that time the place was owned by a contractor, so I got the key to the gate and walked in through a broken window, and was absolutely amazed by what I saw!' In contrast to Castleroy, this fragment remained standing for another thirty years, despite its highly precarious structural state, allowing a fuller record to be made by RCAHMS before final demolition in 1984.

Lithograph of house by D M Walker (from *Nineteenth Century Mansions* **(1958))** (NMRS B41618. Permission to reproduce: Dr D M Walker).

Carbet Castle, view of Dining Room from north-west (1984)   (NMRS A3859).

View of vestibule ceiling (1984)   (NMRS A3881/CN).

Beechwood; view of Drawing Room (1879)
Another late 19th-century Cox house, built for George A Cox to Maclaren's designs. It was purchased by the Corporation in 1934, demolished and the site redeveloped with tenements (NMRS A34004/5. Permission to reproduce: Scottish National Portrait Gallery, Photographic Archive).

View of Grayburn House, Benvie (c. 1920)
An elemental, swept-roofed Arts and Crafts villa built on the western edge of the city in 1907, to the designs of Patrick H Thoms (NMRS AN/3180, B20945; Thoms and Wilkie album).

11–19 North Ellen Street; view of west façade first-floor central window (1989)
This four-storeyed tenement, built by William Webster in 1871, features window surrounds decorated with carved animal and human heads; the architect was John Bruce (NMRS B15834).

Baltic Chambers, 7–11 Bell Street; rear view (1990)
Built *c.* 1850, a typical example of a mid-19th century Dundee tenement, with classical frontage, rear balconies and staircase tower. Each upper floor contains two flats, each of two rooms and kitchen. The name of this tenement is unusual, the term 'chambers' normally being reserved for flatted offices; its use here may result from the block's city-centre location. A WC annexe which formerly stood against the rear staircase tower was removed earlier this century (NMRS B40594).

1–23 Court Street; view from north (1989)
This block, erected in 1874–5 to the designs of David Clunas and the Concrete Building Company, was unusual in two respects: firstly, it was built not by a speculative developer but by a local Working Men's House Building Association; secondly, it was constructed not of stone and brick but of *in situ* mass concrete (NMRS B17783).

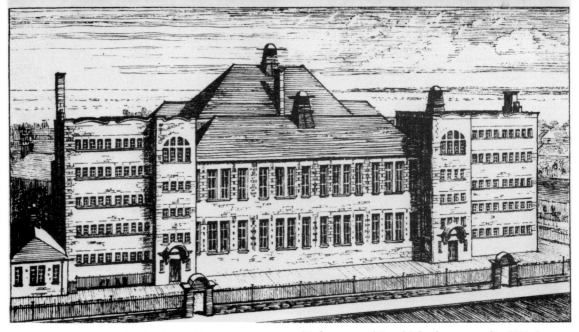

PUBLIC, ECCLESIASTICAL AND COMMERCIAL ARCHITECTURE
Eastern School, Broughty Ferry; drawing by D M Walker (from *Architects and Architecture* (1955))
One of a series of new schools built between 1905 and 1913, this five-storeyed Board School was erected in 1911. It was designed by Langlands, assisted by William Gillespie Lamond and James H Langlands Junior as draughtsmen. The building incorporates steel floor-joists (NMRS B41621; copyright Dr D M Walker).

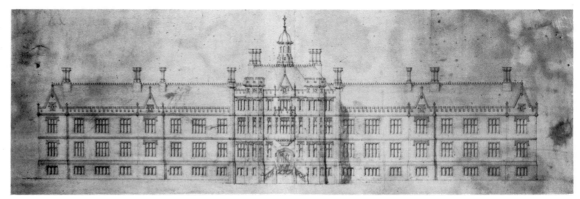

Dundee Royal Infirmary; competition design by Coe and Goodwin
The original block was built in 1853–5 to the collegiate Tudor designs of Coe and Goodwin of London, following a competition. This was the last major Scottish hospital to adhere to the corridor plan (with corridors running alongside the wards) rather than the 'Nightingale' pavilion layout designed to ensure cross-ventilation. This block was extended in 1869 and again in 1910–11; Coe and Goodwin's original Caen stone dressings were replaced by Alexander Johnston, in some cases with slight changes of detail (NMRS AND/268/2. Permission to reproduce: Dundee Art Galleries and Museums).

Eastern Club, 3 Albert Square; view of north façade (1967)

The Eastern Club, a sombre Venetian *tour-de-force* built in 1867–70 to the designs of the architects, Pilkington and Bell, stood on the south side of Albert Square. It was demolished in 1968 (NMRS AN/877).

Albert Institute; photograph by George Washington Wilson (1895)

Albert Square was laid out c. 1862 on drained meadows. The Institute was built in 1865–7 by a private company as a grand memorial to Prince Albert; it was described by its architect, Sir George Gilbert Scott, as '13th and 14th century secular style with the addition of certain Scottish features', presumably including the crow-stepped gables. The building was twice extended in the late 19th century (NMRS AN/2989).

Victoria Royal Arch (1963)

Erected in 1849–50 to the neo-Romanesque designs of J T Rochead, this encrusted archway commemorated the disembarkation of Queen Victoria on a visit in 1844. It was demolished in 1963 to make way for the Tay Road Bridge approach interchange (NMRS AN/201).

St Mary's R C Church, Forebank Road; view from east (1989)
The original church, designed by George Mathewson and built in 1850–1, included the present east gable and barrel-vaulted interior. The vigorous Art Nouveau towers and narthex were added by Thomas M Cappon, with W G Lamond as draughtsman, in 1900 (NMRS B05816).

Bank Street; view from east (*c*. 1890)
The north side of this narrow side-street was built up by various architects between 1859 and 1889 for Sir John Leng, a pioneer of illustrated daily papers. The main Courier Building in Meadowside was also built in 1902. After Leng's death in 1906, the business was taken over by William Thomson, whose firm, D C Thomson, built a four-storeyed print works and office block on the south side of the street after World War II (NMRS B41660).

St Salvador's Episcopal Church; internal view of chancel (*c*. 1900)
Built in several stages between 1857 and 1874 as a mission to Hilltown, this church, with its delicate detailing and rich Pre-Raphaelite interior, seems incongruous in its industrial setting. G F Bodley was responsible both for architectural design and for co-ordination of the internal decorative scheme, largely executed by his own firm, Burlison and Grylls; the furnishings are by Watts and Company. The decoration was restored in 1972 by J and T Harvey with specialist advice from Colin McWilliam and Rab Snowden (NMRS AN/1256).

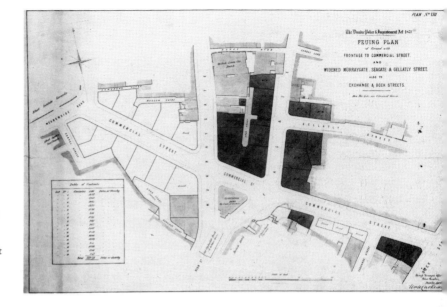

Feuing plan by W Mackison for Commercial Street and Murraygate improvements (1877)
This scheme was the most important part of the redevelopment programme prepared by Mackison under the Dundee Police and Improvement Act 1871. In 1872, the Burgh Surveyor, in consultation with John Lessels of Edinburgh, drew up outline elevations for the new or rebuilt streets, and the component plots were then developed piecemeal to the detailed designs of various architects (NMRS AND/446/3).

73–97 Commercial Street, 15 Meadowside, 2 Murraygate; view from south (1897)
An imposing range of commercial buildings, with busy mixed classical detailing, occupying the north-eastern side of Commercial Street between Meadowside and Murraygate. Built between 1876 and 1892 under the superintendence of various architects, but in accordance with Mackison's guidelines (NMRS B41662. Permission to reproduce; Dundee Public Libraries).

Queen's Hotel; design by Young and Meldrum for north elevation (1875)
This hotel was built in 1878 by W Smith to the Gothic designs of Young and Meldrum. 'A frightening essay in the early French manner Burges had popularised'. . 'clearly drawn by an apprentice desperate to catch the next sitting of the Dean of Guild Court!' (Walker) (NMRS AND/323, B41623).

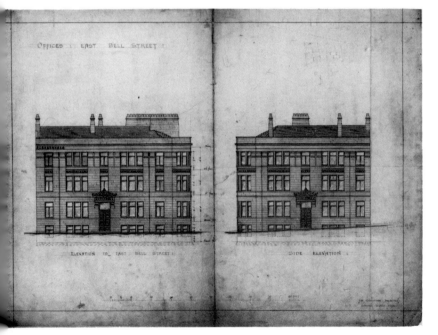

India Buildings, Bell Street; design by J M Robertson for original block (1874)
An office block built for A Hendry in 1874 and extended in 1876. The designs of John Murray Robertson, with their incised geometrical detail, showed a marked resemblance to the work of Alexander 'Greek' Thomson (NMRS AND/57, B41641).

INTERWAR DUNDEE

When World War I ended in 1918, Dundee was unusual among major Scottish cities in that its City Architect and Engineer, James Thomson, had already devised a town plan, comprehensive by the standards of the day. This plan, prepared by 1910 and revised in 1918, envisaged a continuation of Mackison's central area rebuilding, but was now augmented by an extensive suburban road-building programme and, even more important, large-scale slum clearance and building of dwellings for rent by the Town Council. Although municipal house-building as an official, Government-sponsored idea only emerged in 1919 as an unintended consequence of the Government's destruction of the privately rented housing market during the war, Dundee Corporation had already established a Housing and Town Planning Committee in 1907, municipal house-building by the Corporation having first been suggested two years previously. Major boundary extensions to the north and north-east, taking in Broughty Ferry, had also been secured in 1907–14. Accordingly, with a framework already established, the Corporation's programme of development could be started immediately after the war's end. By 1925, the Town Council's work was praised by the *Spectator* as 'a paragon of civic

excellence, whose example other municipalities are asked to emulate'.

In the city's postwar development, housing was regarded as by far the highest priority. In 1919, immediately after the passing of the Housing, Town Planning (Scotland) Act, the Corporation's own building programme was initiated, at Logie. By 1922, 674 dwellings had already been completed. Soon, although there was limited private house-building (including Arts and Crafts or Art Deco villas developed by architects such as Thoms and Wilkie), it had become clear that municipal housing would provide for the vast majority of working- and middle-class demand. By 1939, 73% of all new dwellings built in the city since 1918 had been erected by the Corporation.

Other categories of 'social' building also proceeded apace. Thomson masterminded an ambitious programme of new libraries, designed in a severe Beaux-Arts classical style; school design was allocated to private architects, such as W W Friskin, who produced a series of striking, if lumpish, red-brick schools influenced by contemporary Dutch brick expressionism. But, as this municipal social provision expanded, the city's industry was heading in the opposite direction into stagnation and decline. This trend was most dramatic in the jute industry during the 1930s, where employment dropped from 35,000 in 1929 to 26,000 in 1939 (halving yet again by 1946); by 1931–2 there was 70% unemployment in the industry.

Other traditional industries also declined, but this was slightly offset by expansion in the service industries, which gravitated towards the outermost suburbs, and into planned industrial estates of single-storeyed factories, not altogether unlike the jute works built from the 1870s onwards. The magnet which drew these firms outwards was Kingsway, a ring-road projected by Thomson and initiated soon after the war. During the 1930s, the first industrial estates were built near Kingsway by Dundee Corporation and the Scottish Industrial Estates Corporation; they attracted flourishing firms such as the postcard makers, Valentine, who built a new Kingsway factory in 1937, and the jam manufacturers, James Keiller and Son, who moved from their Albert Square premises to a factory in Lammerton Terrace.

Thomson's plan envisaged the sweeping away of most of the last decaying remnants of the city's mediaeval core by substantial road-widening and construction of a new, classically-planned civic centre. This proposal was progressively realised between 1914 (when building of the Caird Hall was commenced) and 1932–3, when the Town House was pulled down and the new City Square was completed.

The interwar years also saw a boom in commercial building. As there was no shortage of existing offices, shops, hotels and bars, activity in this area mostly took the form of alterations and re-fitting. In the realms of sport and mass entertainment, however, there was much significant new building, including adjacent football stadia north of Dens Road for Dundee FC and Dundee United FC, a new ice-rink beside Kingsway, and various major cinemas such as Green's Playhouse, one of the largest in Europe.

Stannergate, flying-boat hangar; view of east wall of hangar and Curtiss H16 flying-boat (1918)
The former seaplane base at Stannergate was one of several established by the Royal Naval Air Service along the east coast during World War I for reconnaissance and anti-submarine operations. This 'F' type hangar, completed by April 1918, had a metal frame with corrugated-asbestos walls and roof; its east wall was capable of being opened in sections along its entire length. It was demolished in 1983 (NMRS A57307).

Law Hill War Memorial (1989)
The Memorial was built in 1921, its architect, Thomas Braddock of Wimbledon, having won a competition assessed by Sir Robert Lorimer. It comprises a squat granite ashlar tower with cylindrical lantern and bronze brazier (NMRS B05815).

Logie; view from north during construction (1920)
Built between July 1919 and May 1920 to the overall design of the City Architect, James Thomson, this was the first municipal housing scheme to be started in Scotland after World War I. In a conscious reaction against the tenement system and tending towards Garden City planning, 250 collectively-heated dwellings in ungainly blocks were ranged in contoured curves on either side of a tree-lined boulevard. Concerning this central avenue, the Corporation's commemorative brochure in 1920 claimed that 'it is yet too early to appreciate fully the charm of Logie Avenue, but it is not difficult to imagine that when the trees have reached maturity, and the grass has been changed from a feeble green into what Ruskin calls 'that glorious enamel', and flowers fill the air with their sweetness, this majestic thoroughfare will be a thing of beauty and joy for ever to the residenters at Logie' (Copyright: D C Thomson).

Craigiebank: aerial view from south-west (1989)
This garden suburb was laid out in 1919 by James Thomson and his son, Harry, on a concentric plan derived from the Garden City pioneer, Ebenezer Howard. Craigiebank was developed piecemeal by Dundee Corporation and private builders from 1923 onwards when the first 72 Corporation cottages were commenced. The circular area in the middle of this view was originally open amenity land. It was ploughed and cultivated for vegetables during the Second World War, after which flats were erected on it; the church is Frank Thomson's Craigiebank Parish Church, built in 1937 (NMRS B22178).

View of Strathmartine's Lodging and Caird Hall from north (c. 1930)
The first stage in the attempt by the City Architect, James Thomson, to carve out a monumental Beaux-Arts civic centre within the heart of Dundee, was the construction in 1914–22 of the Caird Hall, following a large donation by the industrialist James Caird; this building was described by Colin McWilliam, perhaps a little unkindly, as 'gigantic and architecturally null'. In 1924, Sir J J Burnet designed two north wings, with the intention of forming a grandiose courtyard. In the way of this scheme's realisation stood not only the Town House, but a packed group of 17th- and 18th- century buildings known as 'The Vault', including Strathmartine's Lodging. These buildings, with the exception of the Town House, were demolished in about 1930; construction of the two new wings then proceeded in a pared-down form, amid much Corporation wrangling over the cost of details such as cornices (NMRS AN/20).

Demolition of the Town House

With the new blocks well under construction, the Corporation forced through the demolition of the Town House in 1932, despite last-minute objections from the Ancient Monuments Board. Re-erection of the building elsewhere was suggested, but, although the first stones removed from the spire were numbered, this proposal was abandoned and the building was removed without trace. In a slightly curious commemoration of the 'Pillars', however, two elaborate models were erected above nearby shops in 1932. Following the disappearance of the Town House, the two wings of City Square, containing municipal chambers and shops, were rapidly completed, and the square was opened in 1933.

View of Town House from west during demolition (1932) (Copyright: D C Thomson).

View of Town House ground-floor arcade (*c.* 1930). Traditional meeting-place for generations of Dundonians (Copyright: D C Thomson).

Illuminated copper model of Town House, Crichton Street (1991)
This model was constructed of 1,105 pieces of copper, with electric clock, and was installed above Ross's Bar, Crichton Street, in 1932 (NMRS B40905).

Postcard commemorating opening of City Square (1933) (NMRS B41663).

6

MODERN DUNDEE

In the first twenty-five years after 1945, the Corporation's public housing programme remained by far the most important element in the city's development. Having seen off an attempt by planners to argue for large-scale population dispersal, in the form of the Tay Valley Plan (modelled on the Clyde Valley Plan imposed on Glasgow in 1946), the City began building on extensive boundary extensions it had just secured. At first, in the late 1940s, prefabricated cottages and bungalows were built on outer-suburban sites, and then, during the 1950s, tenements, at locations such as Fintry, Charleston, and Douglas and Angus. The proposed use of multi-storey blocks would enable even more dwellings to be packed on to given sites and allow slum-clearance to be accelerated; such a policy was first discussed by the Housing Committee in 1955 and prototypes were started at Foggyley in 1958. But it was only in the 1960s that large numbers of high blocks were built, mostly on the outer edges of the city but also in a few prominent inner slum-clearance areas. Medium-height 'deck-access' blocks (linked by bridges and walkways) came briefly into vogue in the late 1960s, especially in the vast Whitfield scheme on the city's north-eastern edge.

By this means, the Housing Committee's annual output soared during the 1960s to unprecedented levels, and per head of population was far in excess of any other city in the United Kingdom. By 1966, public housing accounted for 86% of all postwar dwellings in the city, and 44% of its entire dwelling stock; in 1970, Dundee's public housing completions attained an outstanding annual maximum of 2,794. The vital political impetus which made possible this achievement had been provided by three forceful Housing Conveners between 1959 and 1966, all Labour members: Harry Dickson, James Stewart, and Tom Moore. Although controversy later surrounded some of the city's large postwar housing contracts, in retrospect it is clear that 'package deal' schemes were the most rapid and straightforward means of building as many new dwellings as possible in the shortest time.

Construction of other social building-types proceeded apace. Some hospitals were extended while the major Ninewells project was commenced in 1964. Schools were built in large numbers on the peripheral schemes, commencing with prefabricated primary schools in the 1950s and proceeding to traditionally-built primary and secondary schools and nursery schools in the 1960s and 1970s. Higher education development included the building of Further Education colleges and extensions to University College (designated a university in 1967) and to the College of Art; the first architecturally Modern building on the Perth Road campus was the Arts Tower, built from 1959 to Robert Matthew Johnson-Marshall's designs.

Industrial restructuring continued after the war. During the 1950s, jute manufacturers experienced an Indian summer as international trade recovered: substantial investment in re-machining made possible a 55% increase in productivity, and unemployment remained low. Increasingly, there occurred a marked change from the manufacture of packaging to the making of carpet backing. However, the old predominance had gone, with only 18% of employment in the city being textile-related in 1961, compared to 41% in 1931; after 1965, jute output went into final decline, only four firms being left by 1990.

On the other hand, the expansion of the new industries accelerated upon the designation of Dundee as a Development Area under the Distribution of Industry Act 1945. Important new transport links, such as the Tay Road Bridge (1963–6) were forged. The industrial estate programme took hold, attracting major firms such as Timex and National Cash Register to build factories on outer suburban sites in the years immediately after the war: new specialisms, such as office machinery, began to emerge within the city's manufacturing base. By 1966, 90% of postwar industrial development had been located on the industrial estates, and large-scale investment in this area continued with, for instance, the construction of a

national headquarters and warehouse centre for the successful local grocery chain, William Low. City-centre redevelopment also resumed in the late 1950s, taking the form of joint projects between the Corporation, as owner of the land, and nominated developers. The first such scheme was the Overgate redevelopment, built in the early 1960s, followed by the Wellgate project and two smaller areas north of High Street and south of Nethergate.

Thus, during the 1950s and 1960s, Dundee underwent physical restructuring and expansion on a scale which almost rivalled that of the 19th century. In the later 1970s and 1980s, however, there occurred a marked reaction from Modern architecture and sociology, a rejection of newness and exact 'need-fit' planning of buildings and towns, and of demolition and dramatic change. Of course, this was possible only because of the very progress of the earlier campaigns; now the slums had been cleared, and new dwellings by the thousand had been provided.

A very important pointer to this change in local political and public opinion occurred in 1958 when, following a campaign led by Sir Francis Mudie, a proposal to demolish Dudhope Castle was decisively turned down by the Corporation. The Works Committee Convener had advocated the castle's removal, as a 'dilapidated old slum'. But, in striking contrast to the consensus support within the Council for the Town House demolition twenty-six years previously, the proposal was blocked by the votes of key members such as James Stewart, who vigorously opposed demolition as an 'act of vandalism'.

By the late 1980s, clearance of 19th-century tenements had almost ceased. Instead, 'problem'

Playhouse Cinema, Nethergate (1989)
A 4,126-seat 'super-cinema' constructed as Green's
Playhouse in 1934–6 to the designs of J Fairweather, with
interior work designed by John Alexander of Newcastle.
The thrusting steel advertisement tower above the north
façade was clad in sheet metal in 1970. To the rear, the
auditorium block, a vast, humped brick shed, towers over
the Inner Ring Road (NMRS B14220).

'The Clep' public house, Clepington Road (1989)
Built along with two adjacent shops, and designed probably
by the City Architect, J McLennan Brown, in 1941.
Moderne tiled façade with substantially unaltered interior by
Ostler (NMRS B17701).

Dens Park and Tannadice Park football stadia

Dundee's two major football grounds were developed
mainly between the wars, with some large postwar additions.
Dundee FC, founded in 1893, purchased Dens Park in 1919,
and immediately commissioned a remodelling scheme,
including high banking above Dens Road, from the
renowed stadium designer, Archibald Leitch, at a cost of
£60,000. Leitch's stadium opened in 1921, has as its
centrepiece an extensive Main Stand running along its
northern side; in the early 1960s, covers were built on the
South Side Terrace and West End Terrace, and floodlighting
installed. Tannadice Park (formerly known as Clepington
Park) was taken over by Dundee Hibs immediately
following their formation in 1909; the sitting tenants,
Dundee Wanderers, were ejected and razed the existing
stadium to the ground. Renamed Dundee United FC in the
1920s, the club rebuilt and steadily expanded Tannadice
Park between the wars; however, it was only in 1961–2 that
the Main Stand was constructed, a massive L-plan structure
cantilevered out over Tannadice Street and Arklay Street.

**Aerial view from north-west: Dens Park
(foreground); and Tannadice Park (left background)
(1988)**
Between the two stadia are visible the Clepington and
Densfield jute works, both built in 1873–4 (NMRS

**Dens Park Stadium; view of Main Stand from north-
west (1989)**   (NMRS B15842).

council flats at Whitfield were being demolished or reclad, and, following an extensive programme of statutory listing, conversion of redundant jute works to other uses, rather than demolition, was increasingly the norm. Although construction of the last phase of the Inner Ring Road was under way, and further daring improvements to radial roads were under discussion, the chief theme in the city's development was not reconstruction, but environmental improvement.

Menzieshill

As a result of the Corporation's plentiful land supply, most of the Modern schemes of multi-storey and low blocks, built prolifically in the 1960s, were located in the furthest-flung outer suburbs. Menzieshill, three miles from the city centre, includes five 15-storey blocks (9th Development), built in 1963–5 by Crudens.

Menzieshill under construction; view from west, taken from roof of Gowrie Court (1964)
Hillside Court, another high block in 9th Development, is visible on the right. To the left of centre is Charleston Drive; to its north is the completed 5th Development, and to its south are the five-storeyed blocks and terraces of 7th Development, still building (Copyright: D C Thomson).

View of new bus shelter at 351 Charleston Drive (1965)
Construction of dwellings often preceded provision of shops and schools in the new areas by several years, making long bus journeys an everyday necessity (Copyright: D C Thomson).

Menzieshill, Hillside Court; view of laundry (1964)
This view shows Mrs Sharpe, one of the first tenants in this Menzieshill multi-storey block, using the spin-drier. The provision of many up-to-date amenities was taken for granted in Modern multi-storey flats, even in low-rental dwellings (Copyright: D C Thomson).

View of Menzieshill Water Tower (1989)
Reinforced concrete water towers were an essential and prominent feature of large peripheral housing developments on elevated ground. The Menzieshill tower, designed by the Corporation Water Department and opened on 5 September 1963 by the Lord Provost, was built at a cost of £45,000 to serve 1,750 dwellings. Supported by ten tapering reinforced concrete columns, it is 84 feet (26m) high and has a capacity of 160,000 gallons (730,000 litres) (NMRS B17645).

Ardler

One of the most visually striking of Dundee Corporation's outer-suburban schemes of the 1960s. Its centrepiece is an array of six mighty slab blocks, each of 17 storeys and 298 dwellings, built by Crudens as a 'package deal' in 1964–6; this was perhaps Britain's most uncomprising and monumental example of the 'Zeilenbau' pattern of multi-storey blocks in parallel rows. In complete contrast, the scheme also included architecturally *avant-garde* groups of single-storeyed 'patio houses'.

Aerial view from south-west (1988)   (NMRS A55872).

View of supporting columns for slab block under construction (1965)   (Copyright: D C Thomson).

Whitfield

Dundee Corporation's postwar housing drive reached its climax in the huge Whitfield scheme, which included 2,459 deck-access dwellings built by Crudens in 'industrialised' (prefabricated) Skarne construction between 1968 and 1972. These 130 blocks were marshalled in a vast honeycomb pattern of courtyards, now largely broken up by random demolition and application of bright 'vernacular' detail.

Whitfield; view from north-west during construction (1971)
This photograph shows, at foreground and centre, the hexagonal patterns of the Industrialised Phase 1 development, and the two slab blocks of the Central Precinct (built in 1967–8 by Crudens). In the left background, the Industrialised Phase 2 development, comprising further hexagonal courtyards, is seen under construction (Copyright: Aerofilms Ltd).

Whitfield Industrialised Development; perspective of proposed blocks (1967) (Copyright: Crudens Photographic Unit).

Industrialised development, Phase 1; demolition of deck block in progress (1990)
The composite nature of the Skarne 'system', combining *in situ* and prefabricated structural elements, and various types of cladding, is evident here (NMRS B40909).

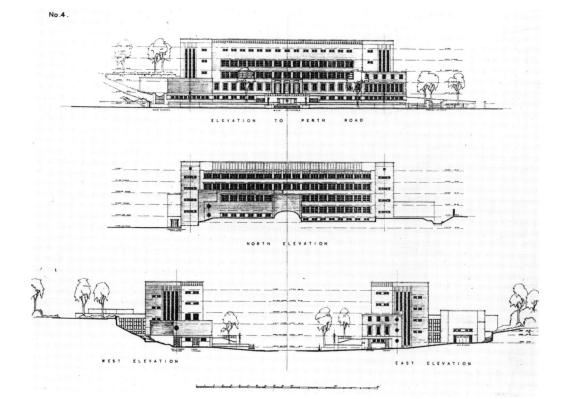

ELEVATION TO PERTH ROAD

NORTH ELEVATION

WEST ELEVATION

EAST ELEVATION

University of Dundee, and Duncan of Jordanstone College of Art
Dundee Technical School and School of Art; commended competition entry by David Carr (1938)
Construction of the winning competition scheme, by James Wallace of Glasgow, was delayed by the war; eventually, it was built in modified form from 1952 onwards. Carr's Kirkcaldy Town House, designed in 1937 and completed in 1956, echoes the modernistic classicism of this unexecuted Dundee design (NMRS B41611; record volume of designs by David Carr).

Duncan of Jordanstone College of Art; view of Matthew Building (1989)
A New Brutalist set-piece by Baxter, Clark and Paul, built in 1974 (NMRS B14385).

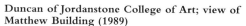

Menzieshill Nursery School (1989)
One of a series of nursery schools built in accordance with a plan launched in 1974 by Dundee Corporation's Educational Committee. These distinctive little buildings are of traditional structure and square plan, with linked play-areas and toplit pyramidal roofs. Because of financial retrenchment during the mid and late 1970s, several were mothballed after their completion. Menzieshill Nursery School, intended to accommodate 90 infants, was built in 1975; after some years of use as a high school annexe and a further period lying empty, it finally opened for its intended purpose in 1983 (NMRS B17046).

Ninewells Hospital and Medical School; aerial view from west (1989)
This 760-bed acute general hospital and medical school was built by Crudens in 1964–74 for the Eastern Regional Hospital Board, to the architectural designs of Robert Matthew Johnson-Marshall. It was seen as a prototype of the policy of 'embedding' (that is, effecting a close interrelation of hospital and medical school), and included, according to the ERHB, 'an architects' and planners' "lab" in which doctors, nurses, architects and planners can conduct life-size experiments with equipment, layout and materials before translating them into the hospital proper'. The hospital was planned in the form of three-storeyed spurs flanking a full-height east-west 'street', with 'racetrack' wards arranged in T-shaped pairs. Construction was broadly traditional, with some precast concrete cladding and low pitched roofs. Although its external architecture cannot be described as daring, the novel organisation and planning of this very large project caused its original completion date to be overshot by five years; its expected cost of £14m was exceeded by nearly two-thirds (NMRS B22142).

Courier Building Extension; view from south-west during construction (1960)
The ten-storeyed extension, designed by T Lindsay Gray, was built in 1958–62. Its remarkable Edwardian Baroque style could be interpreted either as extreme conservatism, fifty years behind the times, or extreme precocity, anticipating Post-Modernism by a quarter of a century (Copyright: D C Thomson).

William Low and Son Ltd Headquarters and Warehouse, Dryburgh Industrial Estate; aerial view from north-west (1989)
From its beginnings in 1868 at a single shop in Ure Street, William Low's grocery business had, by World War I, expanded to include some 75–80 counter shops throughout Scotland. After 1958, the firm embarked upon a vigorous modernisation programme, rapidly phasing in self-service outlets; by 1982, it controlled 43 supermarkets and 17 freezer centres. Forsaking its Bellfield Street site for Dryburgh Industrial Estate (off Kingsway) in 1971–2, the firm built a large headquarters block and 185,000 sq ft (17,250 sq m) central warehouse, one of the largest in Scotland. The architect was K Peers of Egham, Surrey, and the steelwork contractors were Conder (Scotland). During the 1970s, as the firm's business grew still further, the warehouse was enlarged several times (NMRS B22125).

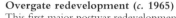

Overgate redevelopment (*c.* 1965)
This first major postwar redevelopment in the city centre was conceived in the mid 1950s and built from 1961 in three stages, beginning at the west with the 'barrier block' of the Angus Hotel beside the Inner Ring Road, and preceding eastwards along an elevated shopping mall towards the terminal feature of a squat office block. The developer selected by the corporation was Murrayfield Real Estate; the contractors were Charles Gray Builders, and the architects Ian Burke, Martin and Partners.

Artist's impression of Phase III (c. 1965)
This view, looking westwards, shows the shops of Phase III with the Angus Hotel in the background (NMRS B40902. Copyright: Ian Burke, Martin and Partners).

View of Overgate before demolition (1954)
(Copyright D C Thomson).

Wellgate redevelopment; view from south-east (1989)
A three-level shopping centre, film theatre and central
library, built in 1974–8 by Caledonian Terminal Securities
(Wellgate) Ltd to the designs of James Parr and Partners, and
financed by Prudential Assurance. Construction of this
massive and controversial contract comprised reinforced
concrete with brown precast concrete cladding and brown
curtain-walling; internally, the 'seventies colour palette of
brown, orange and yet more brown was equally insistent.
The scheme also included a small housing development to
the north-east, designed in a fishing-village vernacular. In
1985–6 the Centre was refurbished by Charles Gray
Builders, James Parr and Partners once more being the
architects (NMRS B14064).

Tay Bridge Station; view from east during rebuilding (1958)
After World War II, while intermittent discussions were pursued about the building of a central bus-railway interchange, Tay Bridge Station assumed progressively greater importance. In 1958, the street-level ticket office and staircase hall was rebuilt in a limp Gibberdian manner, and soon afterwards local steam trains were replaced by Modernisation Plan diesel multiple units. After the closure of East (1960) and West (1965) Stations, all services were diverted to Tay Bridge. The station was again remodelled in the mid-1980s, following the sectorisation of British Railways: the ticket office was clad in beige Hi-Tech sheeting, a walkway and staircase hall were inserted into one corner, and glazed shelters appeared on the island platform (Copyright: D C Thomson).

Omnibus terminal, Seagate/Trades Lane; view of information kiosk (1989)
Dundee's existing 'country bus' station was built in 1958 by W Alexander and Sons (Scottish Bus Group) to replace premises in Lindsay Street. In addition to the appropriately rustic timber and brick terminal building and kiosk, an office block and public and staff waiting rooms were provided (NMRS B14224).

Inner Ring Road, Stage XII; view from north-west during construction (1991)
Here, the final stage of the Inner Ring Road is seen slicing through the Victoria Road area. The contractors were Shanks and McEwan, and the consulting engineer was J F White (NMRS B40904).

Tay Road Bridge

This 42-span bridge was built in 1963–6 and, at that time, was the longest road bridge in Britain. The designers were William A Fairhurst and Partners, engineers, and the main contractors were Duncan Logan of Muir of Ord. The contractors for steelwork erection were Dorman Long, but many of the box girders were fabricated in Dundee by Caledon Shipbuilding and Engineering. In 1966, Colin McWilliam hailed its completion: 'The new Tay Road Bridge swoops down from the Fife hills in a long, continuous slope and finally wheels round in a descending spiral into the centre of maritime Dundee. This will be an even more memorable experience than the first road crossing of the Forth, and surely one of the most dramatic entries into any European city'.

View of navigation channel (1965)

At the top of this view are the permanent box girders spanning the navigation channel near the Fife side; at the bottom, nearly completed, is a 200-foot (61m) temporary opening bridge, suspended from the box girders (NMRS B20859. Permission to reproduce: Tay Road Bridge Joint Board).

View of Dundee approach intersection under construction (1965)

The clutter of the harbour area was erased by a sweeping inverted-trumpet intersection made up of causeways and bridges; here, too, the contractor was Logan (NMRS B20856. Permission to reproduce: Tay Road Bridge Joint Board)

Monument to William Logan, Fodderty Cemetery, Strathpeffer (1982)

In January 1966, the flamboyant contracting tycoon, Willian Logan, chief of Duncan Logan Ltd, was killed when his Piper Aztec aircraft crashed and exploded at Dunain Hill, near Inverness. His curious tombstone reproduces a cross-section of the Tay Road Bridge at its taller and more elegant southern end (NMRS B40906).

SELECT BIBLIOGRAPHY

Intended simply as an illustrative guide to NMRS records relating to Dundee, this work is based on the following selective group of publications, supplemented by reference to the Historic Scotland/Scottish Office Environment Department *List of Buildings of Architectural and Historic Interest*, and by research in Dundee's extensive local history collections (such as the Local History department of the Central Library, the Dundee District Archive and Record Centre, and the District Council's Dean of Guild plans and registers).

Lamb, A C, *Dundee, Its Quaint and Historic Buildings* (1985)

McKean, C, and Walker, D M, *Dundee–an Illustrated Introduction* (1984)

Stevenson, S J, and Torrie, E P D, *Historic Dundee, the Archaeological Implications of Development* (1988)

Walker, B, and Gauldie, W S, *Architects and Architecture on Tayside* (1984)

Walker, D M, *Architects and Architecture in Dundee 1770–1914* (1955: Abertay Historical Society)

Walker, D M, 'The Architecture of Dundee', in Jones, S J (ed.), *Dundee and District* (1968), 284–300

Walker, D M, *Nineteenth Century Mansions in the Dundee Area* (1958)

Watson, M, *Jute and Flax Mills in Dundee* (1990).

ABBREVIATIONS

NMRS: National Monuments Record of Scotland
RCAHMS: Royal Commission on the Ancient and
                   Historical Monuments of Scotland
RIAS: Royal Incorporation of Architects in
                   Scotland
RIBA: Royal Institute of British Architects
SDD: Scottish Development Department
SNBR: Scottish National Buildings Record
SOEnD: Scottish Office Environment Department

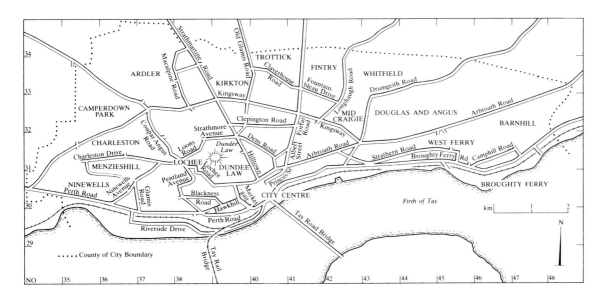

County of the City of Dundee; the pre-1975 burgh